It's another Quality Book from CGP

This book is for 11-14 year olds.

First we stick in all the technical terms
you need to do well in Key Stage Three English.

Then we have a really good stab at
making it funny — so you'll actually use it.

Simple as that.

What CGP is all about

Our sole aim here at CGP is to produce the highest quality
books — carefully written, immaculately presented, and
dangerously close to being funny.

Then we work our socks off to get them out to you
— at the cheapest possible prices.

Contents

Published by Coordination Group Publications Ltd.

Written and illustrated by:
Gemma Hallam
Kate Stevens
Claire Thompson

Additional material by:
Taissa Csáky

ISBN: 978 1 84146 144 1

Groovy Website: www.cgpbooks.co.uk
Jolly bits of clipart from CorelDRAW®
Printed by Elanders Hindson Ltd, Newcastle upon Tyne.

Nouns

A noun is a word that names a <u>thing</u>, like a person, an <u>animal</u> or a <u>place</u>.

Or a vegetable!

Nouns *name* Things

1) *Proper* nouns are for particular things

Hello. I'm Colin.

<u>Proper nouns</u> name a <u>particular</u> person, a <u>particular</u> place, a <u>company</u> or a <u>team</u>, a <u>day</u> of the week or a <u>month</u> of the year. They <u>always</u> begin with a <u>capital letter</u>.

Colin, India, Froggatt's Foods, Thursday, October

Don't forget — your <u>name</u> is a proper noun.
Always write people's names with a <u>capital letter</u>.

2) *Common* nouns are for kinds of thing

These are the common, everyday ones — as you'd expect. <u>Common nouns</u> name a <u>kind</u> of person or thing.

suitcase, hotdog, leaf, woman

3) *Collective* nouns are for groups of things

A <u>collective noun</u> is a word for a <u>group</u> of things.

<u>bunch</u> of flowers, <u>herd</u> of cows, <u>flock</u> of sheep

Common — as muck...

Nouns are words that <u>name</u> things. Nice and easy to start you off. The <u>one</u> tricky bit on this page is the rule about capital letters. Get this into your head — names of actual <u>people</u>, <u>places</u>, <u>companies</u>, <u>sports teams</u>, <u>days</u> and <u>months</u> **ALL** need a **CAPITAL LETTER**.

Singular and Plural

You need to know <u>how many</u> things you're talking about — if it's more than one, you'll probably have to <u>spell it differently</u>, so watch out...

Singular means just One thing

a frog

When there's only one thing, use a <u>singular</u> word.

a sheep

Plural means More Than One thing

It's <u>easy</u> to find the plural of most nouns — you just add **S** on the end.

ten frog<u>s</u>

You <u>can't</u> do all plurals like this, though.

four sheep

If you can make it Plural — it's a Noun

A good <u>test</u> for whether a word is a <u>noun</u> is if you can talk about more than one.

one cabbage ⟶ three cabbages

a went

You can't write this! ⟶ two wents

Watch out, though. There are a few nouns that you can't do this for.

trousers ⟵ These are already plural. It's a pair of trousers, even though it's only one thing.

Plural? — but there's only one Michael Owen...

It's easy to remember that you have to say 'two cats' and not 'two cat'. The next things that need to find themselves a home between your ears are these two words '<u>singular</u>' and '<u>plural</u>'.

SECTION ONE — KINDS OF WORD

Verbs

Verbs are really important words — they tell you what's going on. You need to know how to use them properly, so read on.

A Verb is a Doing word

Doing words are verbs — they're words about doing an action. Verbs tell you what's happening in the sentence. A sentence has to have a verb in it for it to make sense.

Carl likes disco music.

the verb is 'likes'

Being words are verbs too:

Shirley is happy.

the verb is 'is'

Verb Agreement is getting your verbs Right

When the verb and the noun doing the action go together, then they agree. If they don't go together, the sentence won't make sense.

John has buried his dad in the sand.

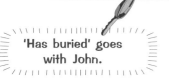
'Has buried' goes with John.

You can't write 'John have buried'!

The Tense of a verb is Past, Present or Future

The tense of a verb tells you when the action is happening.
Verbs can be in the past tense, the present tense or the future tense.

Roberta _fought_ for the rights of vegetables. past

Roberta _fights_ for the rights of vegetables. present

Roberta _will fight_ for the rights of vegetables. future

Roberta, Queen of the Root Vegetables

Verbs tense? — take some deep breaths...

There it is, then — a verb is an action word or a being word. Every sentence has got a verb in somewhere. Think about a verb before you put it in a sentence — it's got to go with the noun that's doing the action. Don't write "you is" or "they wants" or anything daft like that.

Adjectives, Comparatives, Superlatives

These words don't look much fun, but they're not that bad. You can use them for <u>describing</u> things, <u>comparing</u> things, and saying which one is the <u>biggest, smelliest, grumpiest...</u>

Adjectives are Describing words

<u>Adjectives</u> describe <u>nouns</u> and tell you <u>more</u> about them. Adjectives tell you about the <u>size</u>, <u>shape</u>, <u>colour</u> and <u>temperature</u> of things. They show how things make you <u>feel</u>.

Luke was wearing a <u>green</u> jumper.

This tells you <u>more</u> about Luke's jumper.

The monster was <u>huge</u> and <u>scary</u>.

green

huge

scary

This tells you the <u>size</u> of the monster and how it makes you <u>feel</u>.

Comparatives say what's Bigger, Better or Worse

<u>Comparatives</u> are for <u>comparing</u> two things.

comparative

Sarah is <u>taller</u> than Dan.

You add on '-er' to short adjectives.

comparative

Sarah is <u>less cheerful</u> than Dan.

You use 'more' or 'less' with longer adjectives.

Superlatives say what's Biggest, Best or Worst

<u>Superlatives</u> are for <u>comparing</u> lots of things and saying which is the <u>most</u>, <u>least</u>, <u>best</u> or <u>worst</u> out of all of them.

Boris was the <u>fattest</u> cat on the street.

You add on '-est' to short adjectives. Remember, you sometimes have to double the last letter or take off an 'e'.

Soup-erlatives — tastiest, hottest, most oniony...

All these words describe things. If you use them for writing they give a beautifully clear picture of what something's like. It's well worth <u>learning</u> the names — it'll make you sound most impressive.

Adverbs

Adverbs are the '-ly' words that say <u>how</u> something was <u>done</u>. They're very useful for describing what happens in stories and poems and making your writing more <u>interesting</u>.

Adverbs <u>describe</u> Verbs

<u>Adverbs</u> describe <u>verbs</u>. They tell you more about <u>how</u> the action was done. Most adverbs end in <u>-ly</u>. Sometimes adverbs can be a <u>group of words</u>.

The Roland sisters sing <u>beautifully</u>.

This tells you <u>how</u> they sing.

They sing <u>like angels in heaven</u>.

This <u>group</u> of words tells you how they sing.

This tells you <u>how</u> they learnt the new songs.

They <u>quickly</u> learnt two new songs.

Adverbs <u>describe</u> Adjectives

Words like 'totally', 'quite' and 'very' are <u>adverbs</u>. They're used with <u>adjectives</u> to show <u>how much</u> the adjective is working on the noun.

happy

This word is working on the noun.

VERY HAPPY

It's working <u>really hard</u> on the noun now.

a happy dog

a <u>very</u> happy dog

Adverbs — they add to verbs...

<u>Adverbs</u> are words that tell you more about a <u>verb</u> or an <u>adjective</u>. It's easy to remember the word if you think of it as something that '<u>adds</u>' to verbs. You've got to remember they add to adjectives too — that's more tricky, so get it firmly <u>stuck</u> between your ears now.

Little Words

Sentences have teensy little <u>short words</u> as well as nouns, verbs and adjectives. They do lots of different jobs in the sentence. Learn what they're <u>called</u> and what they're <u>for</u>.

Pronouns *do the job of* Nouns

<u>Pronouns</u> stand in for <u>nouns</u> in a sentence to stop you <u>repeating</u> yourself too much.

> *Tanya asked some tortoises to tea.*
> *Tanya gave the tortoises tea and chocolate biscuits.*

Bo-ring.

 This is <u>much better</u> because it doesn't keep repeating the same words.

> *Tanya asked some tortoises to tea.*
> *She gave them tea and chocolate biscuits.*

She makes a lovely cuppa.

'She' stands in for the name Tanya. It's <u>still</u> about her, but it doesn't use her name.

The tortoises are 'them'. You <u>can't</u> write 'gave they'.

Conjunctions *join bits of a sentence* Together

<u>Conjunctions</u> are words like 'and', 'but' and 'then'. They <u>join</u> words together in a sentence. They also join two short <u>sentences</u> together to make one <u>long</u> one.

and and and

> *Iqbal and Tina got up on stage. They sang together.*

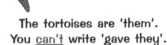 'And' joins the two words together here.

> *Iqbal and Tina got up on stage and sang together.*

 'And' joins the two bits of the sentence together here.

> ...but wait, there's more!
> So, if, while, when, however, because, and though are all conjunctions too.

Little words in sentences — sent, ten, set...

It's easy to forget about the <u>little words</u> in a sentence. They're all important though, so you'd better make sure you <u>know</u> about them — get this lot firmly lodged in your bonce.

Sentences

The thing about a sentence is that it's got to <u>make sense</u>. If you read it and think "Eh? What's going on there, then?", the chances are it's not a proper sentence.

Sentences make Sense on their Own

A sentence can only make sense if it's <u>about</u> something. It can only be <u>about</u> something <u>happening</u> if it's got a verb — that's a good rule to remember. A sentence begins with a capital letter and ends with a full stop, a question mark or an exclamation mark.

The dog wants to go for a walk.

It's about the dog <u>wanting</u> to go for a walk

Bill crept up the stairs.

It's about him <u>creeping</u> up the stairs

A sentence must have a VERB.

The noun and verb Agree — it makes Sense

Getting the verb right is called <u>agreement</u>. The <u>verb</u> has to agree with the <u>noun</u> doing the action.

Catherine thinks about her caterpillars all day.

<u>Catherine</u> is doing the action — the verb is '<u>thinks</u>'.

The caterpillars think about Catherine.

The <u>caterpillars</u> are doing the action — the verb is '<u>think</u>'.

Say it out loud — that's a verb-al agreement

Knowing that sentences have to <u>make sense</u> on their own is more <u>useful</u> that knowing that they begin with a capital letter and end with a full stop. <u>Agreement</u> is just a funny old way of saying that if you don't get your <u>verb</u> right, your sentence will look <u>wrong</u> and it won't make sense.

Phrases and Clauses

Phrases and clauses look a bit confusing at first, but they're just groups of words.
A phrase or a clause is part of a sentence and makes it more descriptive.

A Phrase is a Bit of a Sentence

A phrase is a little chunk of a sentence. It doesn't make sense on its
own, but it tells you a bit more and makes the sentence more interesting.

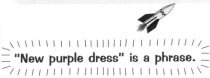
Jade wore her new purple dress.

"New purple dress" is a phrase.

Duncan put his hands in his pockets.

"In his pockets" is a phrase.

A Clause is a Bit of a Sentence with a Verb

The only difference between a phrase and a clause is that a clause has a verb in it somewhere.

Suzy listened to the radio
while she brushed her teeth.

"While she brushed her teeth" is
a clause. It's got a verb in it.
The verb is 'brushed'.

Phrases and clauses Add information to a Sentence

Phrases and clauses describe things. They do the job of adjectives and adverbs. (See P.4-5)

Claude watched television when he got home.

"When he got home" is a clause
doing the work of an adverb.

It tells you when he
was watching television.

He likes programmes about food and drink.

"About food and drink" is a phrase
doing the job of an adjective.

It tells you more about
the programmes.

It's like a cat — really sharp clause...

You can describe things with groups of words. Groups of words that do a describing job are
called phrases and clauses. That's all there is to it, really — not half as bad as you'd think.

Paragraphs

Paragraphs are there to help you — they break long pieces of writing up and make them easier to understand.

A Paragraph is a Group of Sentences

A paragraph is a load of sentences that go together because they're about the same thing. The first line of each paragraph is set in a little way from the margin.

A new paragraph means something's changed.

A new paragraph shows that...
1) A new character has come into the writing.
2) Someone different is starting to speak.
3) The story has moved to a new place.
4) The writing is about a different time.
5) Something really important has happened

Something important has happened.

Someone has started to speak.

Someone else has started to speak.

The story has moved to a new place.

Carol was bored. There was nothing worth watching on the television and nothing worth listening to on the radio.

The phone rang and Carol ran to the kitchen to answer it. It was Nasreen.

"Hi, Caz! Listen, are you busy?" she asked. "Something amazing is happening outside. Come round quickly and have a look," she said, hardly containing her excitement.

"What's happening, Naz?" Carol wanted to know what was going on. She had a feeling that she would have to go and see for herself.

When she got to Nasreen's house, she couldn't believe her eyes. The whole house and the front garden were covered in frogs.

Non-fiction writing uses paragraphs too.

New paragraphs — fresh from the jar...

Paragraphs help you see what's going on when you read a text — and they help other people read what you've written. Now you know all about paragraphs there's no excuse not to use them. If you do it will change your life — well, your writing will be loads better, anyway...

Connectives

If you know about these pesky little things, you'll know how to <u>join</u> clauses and sentences <u>together</u>. Then you can start <u>writing</u> bigger, better, beefier paragraphs.

Connectives join parts of a text

Connectives join <u>clauses</u> together, they link one <u>sentence</u> up with the next, or they start off a new <u>paragraph</u>.

Melissa and I went to the shop

and then

This is a <u>connective</u>. It joins the bits together.

we went to the park

Here's one clause.

Here's another clause.

Connectives do Different jobs

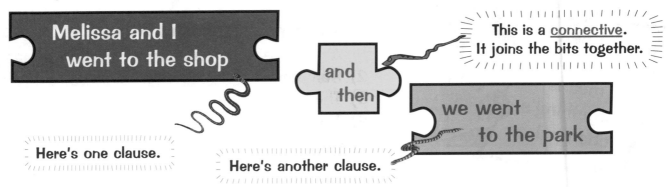

These common connectives are used to say what is going to <u>happen next</u>.

and then

suddenly   just after that

Bill sat down to eat breakfast. Suddenly, his egg hatched.

and

as well as

also

These ones show that the next idea <u>adds onto</u> the first one.

We have two rabbits. Also, we have a cat who eats carrots.

Kirsten had chocolate sauce as well as ketchup on her chips

Disconnected — dial 100 for the operator...

They're just like glue — <u>connectives</u> stick sentences, clauses and paragraphs <u>together</u>. Make sure you learn a few so you can write smooth, flowing text yourself and life will be much brighter...

Punctuation

You know what <u>punctuation</u> is — you've just got to make sure you use it. <u>All the time</u>. Here's the <u>blindingly important</u> stuff you should <u>never forget</u> when you write a sentence.

Start with a Capital Letter

He started to panic.

The ants were here to stay.

Use a <u>capital letter</u> at the start of <u>every sentence</u>.

A Full Stop goes at the end

It's the <u>easiest thing</u> in the world to <u>remember</u>.

Your sentence <u>isn't finished</u> until you've put in the <u>full stop</u>.

It's as <u>simple as that</u>.

Exclamation and Question Marks end sentences too

You use an <u>exclamation mark</u> to show really <u>strong feelings</u>.

"Ouch, that was my foot!"

"Don't jump, Mark!"

You don't need a <u>full stop</u> as well — only the <u>exclamation mark</u>.

You use a <u>question mark</u> if the sentence is a question. <u>Easy</u>.

Where did Lucas leave his cookies?

Remember — <u>no full stop</u> here.

Punctuation — it's a life sentence...

This is straight-down-the-middle kind of stuff, I'd say. It doesn't hurt to get the basics <u>right</u>, though, so test yourself on <u>each heading</u> to make sure you really know it. Easy peasy.

Commas

Commas are <u>easy</u> to put in, but <u>tricky</u> to get <u>right</u>. Learn this stuff.

Commas **are used in** Lists

You've done this before, but it's worth remembering. A <u>comma</u> goes after every word in the list except the <u>second last one</u> and the <u>last one</u>. Put '<u>and</u>' or '<u>or</u>' between the last two words.

The foxes wore trainers, ties, hats and sunglasses.

comma

Commas **mean there's something** New **coming**

If you've got <u>two different ideas</u> in your head when you think of your sentence, you need a <u>comma</u> in between them.

This is one idea.

This is a new idea.

The squirrel pounced...

comma

...frightening the giraffe.

When you're reading, <u>pause</u> a little bit to show that there's a new part to the sentence.

The two little pictures go together as one sentence

The squirrel pounced, frightening the giraffe.

Comma

<u>Comma thieves — in for a long sentence...</u>

<u>Two</u> big juicy things about commas here, then — now get them <u>learned</u>. Commas in <u>lists</u> are pretty <u>easy</u>. Just don't forget that a comma also goes between <u>two ideas</u> in a sentence.

SECTION THREE — PUNCTUATION

Speech Marks

Speech marks are the two pairs of little squiggles we put around text to show when somebody is talking.

Speech Marks show when someone is Speaking

Speech marks go before and after the words which are spoken:

Speech marks open the actual speech.

Speech marks close it again.

"A little bit of custard never hurt anyone," Agnes said.

The first spoken word always has a capital letter.

Burt asked, "Do you think the pizza is ready?"

Capital letter

When people Speak you start a New Paragraph

Every time someone starts speaking, you start a new paragraph.

New paragraph every time someone new speaks.

> The giraffe ran into the room and hid behind Peter.
> "What's the matter?" Peter asked the quivering creature.
> "The squirrel is after me again," the giraffe sobbed. "Don't let it get me!"

Don't need a new paragraph here because it's the same person talking.

Speech marks — the Queen gets 10 out of 10...

Put speech marks when someone starts to speak, and then when they finish and Bob's your uncle. Make sure you always start a new paragraph when someone new speaks — and don't forget those all-important capital letters for the first spoken word. Get it into your head and keep it there.

Apostrophes

Eeek! That's a <u>scary-looking</u> word. I don't know why you need such a long word — they're just little squiggles used for <u>punctuation</u> after all.

Apostrophes make Two words into One

An <u>apostrophe</u> is popped in where letters are taken out:

letter taken out | apostrophe put in

Who is → Who ₁s → Who 's

letters taken out | apostrophe put in

We have → We ₕₐve → We 've

Check out these beauties —

It is	———	It's
I am	———	I'm
did not	———	didn't
they are	———	they're
let us	———	let's

Apostrophes show Who owns What

① To show that something <u>belongs</u> to a person, you take their name and add an <u>apostrophe</u> and an 's'.

add 's

Paul → Paul's things

Paul's nose

Paul's cupcake

The Bats.

add '

The Bats' Binoculars.

② If it's a <u>group</u> of people or things which ends in 's', all you do is <u>stick an apostrophe on the end</u>.

Apostrophe — what a catastrophe...

<u>Two</u> juicy tidbits about apostrophes here — ready for you to <u>soak</u> up. Apostrophes go where letters are <u>taken out</u> when two words get joined together. They also show who <u>owns</u> what — make sure that bit about <u>groups</u> of things that end in '<u>s</u>' is firmly stuck in your noggin.

More Punctuation

Some more exciting punctuation marks for you to look out for — learn and enjoy.

Colons and Semi-colons mean Pauses

If you see a <u>colon</u> or <u>semi-colon</u> when you're reading <u>pause</u> before reading the next part.

To make scones you need: flour, butter, water and salt.

Read this bit first.   Then read this part.

PAUSE

Through the magnifying glass we saw the eyes of the ladybird; the spider's fangs; and the weevil's chomping jaws.

PAUSE   **PAUSE**

Dashes also show you where to Pause

<u>Dashes</u> are short lines which are often used to mark a <u>dramatic pause</u> in a sentence.

We thought Chris was normal — until he showed us his feet.

PAUSE

Hyphens join words Together

<u>Hyphens</u> are used to <u>link words</u> to make the meaning clear.

...add a hyphen...

A man eating squid.   *A man-eating squid.*

Big pause — that's what bears have...

<u>Watch out</u> for these little tricksters, they're all over the place. <u>Colons</u>, <u>semi-colons</u> and <u>dashes</u> all mean the same thing when you're reading out loud — make sure you <u>pause</u> before you read the next bit. If you stick a <u>hyphen</u> between two words you can change the whole meaning.

Word Building

There's definitely more to these funny <u>word</u> things than meets the eye. Take one ordinary, boring word, <u>stick an extra bit on it</u> — and bingo! You've got yourself a <u>different word</u>.

The Root Word is what you Start with

The <u>root word</u> is the main idea.

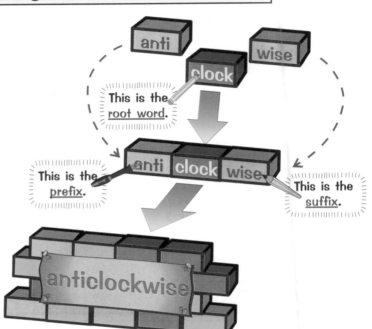

This is the <u>root word</u>.

This is the <u>prefix</u>.

This is the <u>suffix</u>.

anticlockwise

Clump it together as <u>one word</u>. There's <u>no need</u> for a <u>hyphen</u>.

A Prefix goes at the Front

You put a <u>prefix</u> at the <u>start</u> of a root word. These are all prefixes:

ground ➤ underground

This bit's the <u>prefix</u>.

under mis de ex pre anti un re sub

Wow — there are <u>bags</u> of them...

A Suffix goes at the End

The <u>suffix</u> is the part you add to the <u>end</u> of words.

ish ed er ing ment

Truckloads of them...

This bit's the <u>suffix</u>.

garden ➤ gardener

Root words? — I thought you said rude words...

It's pretty clear what this page is about — making new words by <u>adding</u> onto old ones. The tricky bit is remembering <u>prefix</u> and <u>suffix</u>. They always seem to have <u>silly</u> names for things.

Same, Opposite and Mini

They just keep coming up with big words to talk about simple things.
Here are three more — learn what they mean and don't forget.

Synonyms are words that mean the Same

Words like "big" and "large" are synonyms — they mean the same thing.
Synonym is bit of a daft name, but that's what they're called, so you're stuck with it.

These are synonyms for
the word scared...

frightened,
petrified,
terrified

Sarah was scared. She was wearing Arthur's
kennel again and she knew he'd be cross.

angry, furious,
annoyed

... and these are synonyms
for the word "cross".

Antonyms are Opposites

Opposite words are things like "hot" and "cold" — and they're called antonyms.
You can use some prefixes and suffixes to make antonyms:

Prefixes like these
make opposites:

anti un mis
dis in non

happy → unhappy

Add ful and less to a root word
and you get two opposite words.

care → careful
            careless

Diminutives shrink things

Diminutives are words that make things sound small. You could add a suffix like kin, let or y on
the end of a word...

pig → piglet

Jane → Janey

...or put another word before it, like little.

little Jane

Help me — I think I'm shrinking...

Don't get antonyms and synonyms muddled up — remember: synonym = same. Diminutive is
a silly big word for a simple thing — you just use them to make things sound small.

Word Patterns and Pictures

Uh-oh... even <u>more</u> scary-looking words coming up — <u>luckily</u> they aren't half as bad as they sound. This page is just about things that <u>pep up</u> writing so that everyone will <u>want</u> to read it.

A <u>Simile</u> <u>says things are</u> <u>Like Each Other</u>

A <u>simile</u> is a way of <u>describing</u> something by saying it's <u>like something else</u>.

> The purple hat thief crept up <u>as quietly as a mouse</u>.

> This is a <u>simile</u>. It tells you <u>how quiet</u> the thief was.

Instead of this

... you picture this.

<u>Alliteration</u> <u>repeats the</u> <u>Same Sounds</u>

When you use lots of words that <u>start</u> with the <u>same sound</u>, it's called <u>alliteration</u>.

> Tom *t*ickled the *t*iger's *t*ummy.

Use <u>alliteration</u> for <u>short snappy slogans</u> in adverts and leaflets — it works a treat.

<u>Onomatopoeia</u> — <u>Sounds Like</u> <u>what it's talking about</u>

Some words <u>sound</u> a bit <u>like the noise</u> they're talking about — that's called <u>onomatopoeia</u>.

> Words like these give you <u>really cool effects</u> in your writing.

> The car <u>screeched</u> to a halt.

> "<u>Crunch</u>" went Jamie's bike, as he <u>smashed</u> into the car.

Similes — they're like mixed up smilies... ☺

<u>Three</u> great ways to <u>improve</u> your writing — nobody wants to read something which is <u>dull</u> and <u>boring</u>. Learn them so you can <u>grab</u> the reader and make them really <u>understand</u> what you mean.

Homophones and Puns

Spelling gets a bit tricky when words sound the same, so you'd better watch out. Of course, you wouldn't be able to make all those side-splitting puns if some words didn't sound alike...

Homophones are words which Sound the Same

Homophones are words that mean different things, but sound the same.

This is a postage stamp.

Look at the rest of the sentence to work out which word it means.

"Don't stamp on my ketchup sandwich!"

Jenny let out an enormous wail. She couldn't find her bear anywhere.

WAAHH!

Willy

Jenny let out an enormous whale. It would be free at last.

You'll sometimes need to look at the sentence after that as well.

A Pun is a Play on Words

WORDS

A play on words — get it...

Using words and phrases that sound the same to make a joke is called making a pun.

I'm on a seafood diet — I see food and I eat it.

Seafood is things like fish and prawns.

When he sees food, he eats it.

Newspapers use puns to make eye-catching headlines.

ho ho

This one plays on the words hare and hair.

Metro News
Where's my bunny?
Man's tragic hare loss

Total joke eclipse — don't look at the pun...

There are lots of tricky words which sound the same as other words but are spelt differently. It'll help you loads if you learn them — and then you can make side-splittingly funny puns too.

Fact, Fiction and Non-Fiction

Text, fiction and non-fiction — all sounds a bit technical to me. It's not that bad really, they're just fancy words used for different kinds of writing. You do need to know them, so read on.

Text is Any kind of Writing

Text means stuff that's been written down. Stories, articles, letters and instructions are all different kinds of text.

You'll come across this word a lot — so make sure you know it.

Fiction is Not Real

Fiction is stuff like stories, plays and poems.

Everything is made up by the writer.

The people and the things that happen are imaginary, but it could be set somewhere real.

Non-fiction is Real life

Non-fiction is writing about the real world. It's writing that isn't made up.

That's things like:

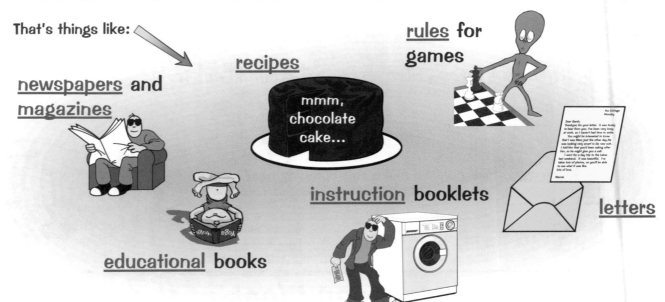

newspapers and magazines

recipes

mmm, chocolate cake...

rules for games

educational books

instruction booklets

letters

Fact, Fiction and Non-Fiction

Here's some more stuff about <u>writing</u>. Hang on in there — it won't take long, I promise.

Fact is not the same as Opinion

<u>Facts</u> are <u>true</u>. That's pretty simple.

If you can <u>prove it</u>, it's <u>fact</u>.

"The capital of Spain is Madrid."

FACT

SPAIN
■ Madrid

You can look it up in an encyclopaedia.

<u>Opinion</u> is what <u>someone thinks</u>.

Other <u>people</u> might <u>disagree</u> with your <u>opinion</u>.

"Football is better than television."

OPINION

Not everyone thinks so.

Narrative tells a Story

<u>Narrative</u> tells you the <u>events that happened</u> in the <u>right order</u>. It could be <u>fiction</u>, or something that <u>really happened</u>.

Narrative can be <u>written</u>...

... or it can be <u>spoken</u>.

(<u>stories</u> and <u>poems</u>)

Wasp fiction — a sting in the tale...

Two lovely pages about <u>writing</u>. It might seem like a lot to learn, so make sure you <u>understand</u> the information under <u>each heading</u> before you go onto the next one and <u>you'll be fine</u>.

Different Kinds of Fiction

There are loads of different kinds of stories — all with their own different styles. Read on to find out more about the amazing tales we tell.

Myths are Ancient Stories

Myths are made up stories about gods or heroes. They've been told since ancient times to explain things like why the sun rises or why it rains.

> Myths are completely made up.

> There is a myth that the Sun God sailed across the sky every day, carrying the sun on his ship.

Legends are tales of Real Heroes

Legends are traditional stories based on real people. Most of them started out as true stories, but things have been added over the years.

King Arthur did exist...   but there was no lady in the lake.

REAL MADE UP

A Fable is a story with a Moral

Fables are short tales like "The Hare and the Tortoise" which make a point — called a moral.

> A hare and a tortoise are having a race. The hare thinks he'll easily win, so he has a rest and falls asleep. Meanwhile, the tortoise overtakes and wins the race.

> The moral of the story is:
> If you try you will succeed;
> if you're lazy you'll lose out.

Jesus told Parables

and some fell on stony ground...

Fables are sometimes called parables. Jesus told parables to his disciples to help them understand what he was teaching them.

Uh oh — been caught telling stories again...

You must admit — stories are fun. The different names can be a bit confusing at first, especially the difference between myths and legends. Remember that myth means totally made up.

Different Kinds of Fiction

Stories are not boring — no way. They can be about all sorts of weird and wonderful things. Here are three kinds of story you're bound to have come across.

Fairy Tales are children's stories

Fairy tales are stories written for children. There are hundreds of them, but you can spot the same ideas in all of them:

1) good defeating evil,
2) a happy ending.

Hansel and Gretel, Rapunzel... you've heard them all before.

Fantasy adventures are Magical

Fantasy adventures are stories where magic happens. You could be in an imaginary world with witches and elves... or you could be somewhere totally ordinary, but with really weird things happening.
In other words...

if your teacher turns into a fire-breathing hamster in the middle of a Maths lesson...

... or you're sitting in a magic tree with a pixie,

— it's a fantasy story.

Science Fiction is usually set in the Future

Science fiction stories are about space, aliens or time travel. Just think of things like Star Wars and Star Trek.

They're often set in the future.

A long time ago, in a galaxy far, far away...

Stories can be about all sorts of things — just take a look in your library. I bet you've read stories like these before, now you just need to learn all the nitty gritty details.

Looking Things Up

These are all different places where you can look things up to find <u>information</u> about words. <u>Watch out</u> — the names can be a bit tricky to spell.

A <u>Dictionary</u> tells you what words <u>Mean</u>

You can <u>look up any word</u> in a dictionary and find out <u>what it means</u>.

squelch *v.* walk with wet sucking sound, as in walking through mud. *n.* sound that this makes.

It's in <u>alphabetical order</u>. Dead easy.

A <u>Glossary</u> explains <u>Difficult</u> <u>words</u>

A <u>glossary</u> is a <u>list of difficult words</u> and what they <u>mean</u>.

A <u>glossary</u> is like a <u>mini-dictionary</u>.

If the writer thinks you <u>won't</u> <u>understand something</u>, it goes in the <u>glossary</u>.

A <u>Thesaurus</u> helps you <u>Find Different Words</u>

<u>Look up a word</u> in a <u>thesaurus</u> — and you'll find loads of <u>other words</u> that <u>mean the same</u> thing.

cold arctic, bitter, chilly, cool, freezing, frosty, frozen, wintry

For the last time, my name's <u>Tyrannosaurus</u> — not <u>Thesaurus</u>.

Use a <u>thesaurus</u> to find <u>better</u> <u>words</u> to use in your <u>writing</u>.

Words that mean the same thing are called <u>synonyms</u> (see P.17)

An <u>Encyclopaedia</u> is full of information

An <u>encyclopaedia</u> is full of <u>information and pictures</u> about <u>all kinds of subjects</u>.

Encyclopaedias are always in <u>alphabetical order</u> — so to find the <u>capital of China</u> you'd look up China in the <u>C section</u>.

China
Capital: Beijing
Population

Thesaurus — isn't that an extinct species...

The names are a bit <u>grim</u>, I admit, but all you need to know is how you use each one. Use a <u>dictionary</u> and a <u>thesaurus</u> to look up words as you go along — your writing will be stacks better. You can find all sorts of fascinating facts in an <u>encyclopaedia</u>, so go on, dive in and enjoy.

Looking Things Up

Here's some stuff about books that is <u>seriously</u> important. Learn this and you'll be able to <u>zip around</u> books without getting bogged down in pages and pages of <u>words</u>.

Contents tell you What's in a book

The <u>contents</u> page is at the <u>front</u> of the book. It tells you <u>where each section starts</u>.

The <u>contents</u> page lists things <u>in the order</u> they come <u>in the book</u>.

Contents

Section One
Cats in History 1-4
Famous cats 5

Section Two
Looking After your Cat 6-8
Going to the Vet 9

Section Three
Breeds of cat 10-14

Contents

Section Four
Teaching your cat to read 15-16
Maths for cats 17-18

The Index tells you Where to Find Topics in a book

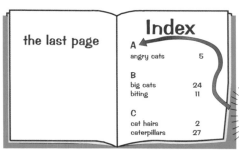

the last page

Index

A
angry cats 5

B
big cats 24
biting 11

C
cat hairs 2
caterpillars 27

The index lists the <u>important</u> words in <u>alphabetical order</u>.

The <u>index</u> is at the <u>back</u> of the book. When you <u>look up a word</u>, it tells you <u>which pages</u> to read.

A Bibliography is a List of Books

Yeah, it's a <u>big scary word</u>, but that's all it means — a list in the <u>front or back</u> of a book.

There are <u>three kinds</u> of <u>bibliography</u>:

1) a list of <u>books</u> the <u>author used</u>,
2) a list of <u>books</u> on the <u>same subject</u>,
3) a list of <u>books</u> by the <u>same author</u>.

That's all there is to it.

Be contented with this lot...

These are three pretty <u>similar</u> things and they all help you <u>look stuff up</u>. Bibliography is a horrible long word — I don't know why they can't just call it 'a list of books'. All you've got to do here is <u>learn</u> what these little tricksters <u>do</u> and where to find them, and it'll all fall into place.

Reading Plays

Plays are a bit strange to read — they're always more fun to watch, I reckon. Still, you can't get out of it. Here's everything you ever wanted to know about playscripts...

Playscripts are meant to be Acted Out

A playscript is the script for a play. It's written to be acted out on stage.
The playscript has all the instructions for how to perform the play, including:

> Where each scene is set,
> what's happening on stage,
> what the actors say.

Can't I say something other than "woof"?

Plays are split into scenes. Each time there's a new time or place, a new scene starts.

Almost The Greatest Play In The World Ever
Act One

Scene One

(Wigan, 1987, a secret underground cave, there is a time machine and chemical jars are scattered around. The lights come on as Vic the mad professor enters.)

Vic: (To himself.) Ha ha — one more squirt of turnip juice and my time machine will be complete.

(PC Parsons bursts in)

PC: Oh no you don't! I'm arresting you for the theft of one turnip!

These bits in brackets are the Stage Directions.

They say what the stage looks like and tell you about lighting and stuff.

They also tell you when the actors enter the stage.

These are the lines the actors say.

This is how the actor should say this line.

Acting — a great excuse to cause a scene...

Playscripts look a bit odd at first — they seem like all talk and no story. But really the actors tell the story by acting it out. Remember not to read the stage directions out loud, they're there to tell the actors what to do and how to say their lines so they can make the play believable.

Riddles and Tongue Twisters

Riddles and tongue-twisters are tops I reckon — more fun than you can poke a stick at.

A Riddle is a Clever Question

A riddle is a question that's been worded so that you can't tell straight away what it means.

> What goes on four legs, then two legs, then three?
> Answer my question and you will go free.
> Answer it quickly or sorry you'll be.

The answer to this one is a human being. We crawl on all fours when we're babies, then we learn to walk on two legs. When we're old we walk with a stick (three legs).

Tongue-twisters are Hard to say

Tongue-twisters have got lots of similar consonant sounds, and they all get horribly mixed up when you try to say them quickly. That's why...

tongue-twisters are tricky to twist your tongue round.

This keeps repeating the sounds t, tw and tr — wouldn't want to try that with a mouthful of food...

red lorry, yellow lorry,
red lorry, yellow lorry

r l
y

That fat thrush flew
through the thorny thicket.

th f
thr fl

Tongue-tied — tired twister ties tongue to tonsils ...

I'd say you've come across these before — don't skip this bit though, you do actually need to know how they work. See if you can come up with your own riddles and tongue-twisters.

Writing a Story

Whether you're <u>writing</u> a story or <u>reading</u> one, you could do with knowing these three things.

The <u>Plot</u> <u>is</u> <u>What</u> <u>Happens</u>

The <u>plot</u> of a story is all the things that happen, in the <u>right order</u>.

 Beginning

 Middle

 End

A plot needs a beginning, a middle and an end.

The <u>Setting</u> <u>is</u> <u>Where</u> <u>it</u> <u>Happens</u>

<u>Where</u> it happens makes a difference to <u>what</u> happens.

A horror story could be set in an old haunted house.

Scary things will happen in a story like this.

The <u>Theme</u> <u>is what it's</u> <u>About</u>

For example, the <u>theme</u> of most fairy tales is <u>good</u> against <u>evil</u>. The good characters <u>always</u> win in the end.

Good
v
Evil

Cinderella got to go to the ball and marry the prince, and her ugly sisters didn't get what they wanted.

Remember, remember the fifth of November...

The words might be <u>new</u>, but what they mean is nice and simple. Plot, setting and theme are things that <u>all</u> stories have got. You need to spot them and say how they work — so <u>learn</u> them.

Telling a Story and Dialogue

Who's <u>talking</u> in a story is pretty important. You need to know who's <u>telling</u> the story, and understand what's going on when people <u>speak</u> in a story.

The <u>Narrator</u> is the Person <u>Telling</u> the story

I carefully opened the jar and spread the jam over my head.

The narrator <u>is</u> in the story.

Peter and Pippa played in the snow.

The narrator <u>isn't</u> in the story.

<u>Dialogue</u> is when people <u>Speak</u> in a story

Speech in a story needs <u>speech marks</u> to show where it starts and stops.

 Dialogue lets you know what's happening.

Question marks and exclamation marks let you know that Lucy is upset and Danielle is asking a question.

"Oh, no!" cried Lucy.
"What's up?" asked Danielle.
"The box isn't here!"said Lucy, in a panic. "It's gone!"

The characters are talking to each other about what's <u>happening</u> in the story.

The narrator doesn't <u>need</u> to say that the box had gone missing — you <u>know</u> that from what Danielle and Lucy have said.

Story writing — a good excuse for telling tales...

The <u>narrator</u> can be <u>in</u> the story or they can be telling the story about <u>someone else</u>. <u>Dialogue</u> is a fancy word for when people <u>talk</u> — it's amazing how a bit of speech helps move a story along.

Who Is It For?

You're probably used to writing things for your teacher and thinking no more of it. You'll find it really helps if you think about <u>who</u> a text is for and <u>why</u> it's written when you're reading or writing.

The <u>Audience</u> are the <u>People</u> <u>you're writing For</u>

<u>Audience</u> doesn't just mean the people watching, like a play or a pantomime.
Your <u>audience</u> means the people who are going to <u>read</u> your writing.

Different people need different kinds of writing.

It says here that pigs can't read

Your <u>Purpose</u> — <u>it's the Reason</u> <u>for writing</u>

You could be writing a thank-you letter to your <u>Grandma</u> for your birthday present, or a letter with a <u>totally different purpose</u>, <u>complaining</u> about a faulty computer game.

PURPOSE — to thank Grandma for the slippers, to say that you like the slippers and to say that you have been wearing them

PURPOSE — to say what you bought, to say what is wrong with it, to say that you are disappointed and to ask for a new one

6 Windsor Grove, Newhampton

Dear Grandma,
Thank you very much for the bunny rabbit slippers. They are very cute. They fit me perfectly, and I have been wearing them all day. Everyone says that pink suits me.

Lots of love,

Harry

Casual chatty language.

6 Windsor Grove, Newhampton

Dear Sir,
Yesterday I bought "Graverobbers 2". I had read about the game in a computer magazine and I was looking forward to playing it.
 I was very disappointed to find that I could not install the game on my computer. When I clicked 'yes' on the install menu, error code E0001035 appeared on screen. I tried restarting my computer, but the same thing happened again.
Please could you send me a new copy of the game? I have enclosed my receipt as proof of purchase.

Yours faithfully

H. Dixon
Harry Dixon

Formal language and long words.

Be like a dolphin — know your porpoise...

The point of all this is that there are <u>loads</u> of different ways of writing. The way you write depends on <u>what</u> the writing is <u>for</u> and <u>who's</u> going to <u>read</u> it. <u>Think</u> about it, it makes <u>sense</u>.

Putting It Together

The <u>order</u> that things go in is very <u>important</u>. If your writing is all jumbled up, it won't make any <u>sense</u>. This lovely page shows you how it works.

Sequence *is the* Order *of things*

<u>Instructions</u> have to follow the right <u>order</u> or they won't make sense.

This is in the wrong order! You have to break the eggs before you can add them to the mixture.

Fairy Cakes.

1. *Beat butter with the sugar until fluffy.*
2. *Add the eggs and mix well.*
3. *Break two eggs into a bowl.*
4. *Add the flour and baking powder and stir gently.*

Structure *is how it's all* Put Together

It's nice and <u>easy</u> to read writing that's been put together well. If you know how different types of writing are <u>laid out</u> on the <u>page</u>, you can use those layouts in your own writing.

A letter has the address of the person writing in the top right hand corner.

Newspapers have columns to make them easier to read.

Bill Jones
Ivy Cottage
Liston

Dear Mrs Lewis,
Thankyou for your letter.

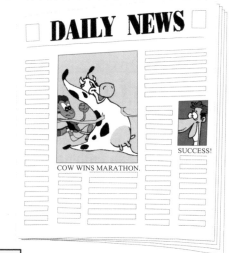

Timetables are arranged in columns to help you see what bus or train to catch.

Broughton	1045	1215
Grizebeck	1056	1226
Ulverston	1115	1232

Subheadings *are like* Mini-titles

On this page, there is a <u>main heading</u> 'putting it together' and three <u>subheadings</u>. The subheadings give you a better idea of what to expect on the page.

Sequence — mum sews them to my leotards...

Good <u>layout</u> helps all the information soak into your brain — look at the way this book is laid out for maximum <u>facts-into-head</u> transfer. The bit about <u>sequence</u> and order is nothing more than simple <u>common sense</u> really, so I don't want to see you getting it wrong. Learn and enjoy.

Discussion, Debate and Editorial

There's nothing like a good _discussion_ to get you thinking. Read on to find out about how people put their _opinion_ in _writing_.

A _Discussion_ is about a _Tricky Topic_

A discussion could be in letters to a newspaper _arguing_ about something in the news, or in a book about something that _not everyone agrees on_.

A _Debate_ goes through points _For_ and _Against_

A _debate_ is a kind of discussion. It goes through all the points _for_ and _against_.

A long involved discussion between two points of view is a debate.

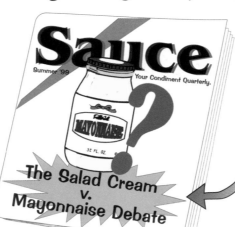

Sauce
Summer '99   Your Condiment Quarterly.

The Salad Cream v. Mayonnaise Debate

What people say in a debate is _opinion_ — it's what they think.

Some people prefer _salad cream_, some people prefer _mayonnaise_.

An _Editorial_ gives _Opinion_

You'll find _editorials_ in newspapers. They tell you what the newspaper _editor_ thinks about something happening in the _news_.

A newspaper editorial is _opinion_ because it's what someone _thinks_, and there isn't usually much _evidence_ to back up what's written.

This Paper says
Throw out this Stupid Law

The crazy new chip law must go!
Who do these barmy politicians think they are?
British chips have been long and square for as long as we can remember. We don't want triangular chips, and we won't have them.

Discussion — goes on dis sofa...

This whole page is about putting _points of view_ into writing. A _discussion_ tackles subjects which people _disagree_ about. It's all about getting both sides of the story. _Editorials_ are a chance for _newspapers_ to speak out — if you don't agree you can always wrap your chips in them.

Persuasive Writing

Have you ever been sure that you're right and nobody else believed you?
Well, this is what this page is all about, <u>making people believe</u> what you say.

Persuasive writing gives a Point of View

Writing that tries to <u>persuade</u> people of a point of view is called
<u>persuasive</u> writing, which seems fairly <u>obvious</u>.

Work out what you want to say as a <u>list of points</u>.
Here's an example about school uniform.

1) *School uniform is outdated.*

2) *You can't be individual in school uniform.*

3) *People should be allowed to wear what they like.*

4) *School uniform isn't necessary.*

Get them into the right <u>order</u>, so they kind of follow on from each other.

The Argument is what you're trying to say

The point you're making is called your <u>argument</u>. The important thing
is putting your argument across so that <u>everyone</u> will <u>agree</u> with it.

But I don't get it...

Everyone knows that...

These are all ways of convincing
people that you're right.

Even a fool could see that...

Even a farmyard animal would understand...

I'm always right — why won't you admit it?

Important stuff this — there's nothing worse than people not believing a word you say. Even if
you're <u>sure</u> about your <u>argument</u>, you still need good <u>writing</u> skills to make other people agree
with you. An argument <u>doesn't</u> mean a fight here, it's all the <u>points</u> you're trying to make.

Key Words — Important Phrases

You'll have to agree — it's much easier to remember <u>key points</u> than a whole lot of words.

Key Words **are the** Most Important Words

The <u>key words</u> in a sentence or a paragraph give you the real <u>nitty-gritty</u> of the meaning.
The other words add a few frills and detail, but aren't absolutely essential.
Here's an <u>example</u> from a newspaper article to show how it works.

Warm-hearted Salworth schoolchildren have raised over £2000 for the Kosovan refugee appeal by holding a series of coffee mornings in the school hall.

You can pick out 'schoolchildren', '£2000', 'refugee appeal' and 'coffee mornings' here

Key Phrases **are the** Most Important Phrases

You don't need to remember every single word of a bit of writing to remember what it was about. <u>Key phrases</u> tell you what it's getting at.

Lions are big cats that live in the African savannah. The male has a distinctive mane of thick fur on his neck. The female does most of the hunting. Her prey can be antelope, zebra and wildebeeste. Lions live in large family groups called prides.

These phrases are the important ones: big cats; live in Africa; male has mane; female hunts antelope, zebra and wildebeeste; group of lions called a pride.

If you really want to remember a piece of information, <u>underline</u> the <u>key phrases</u> and write them down as <u>notes</u>. It's a lot <u>better</u> than learning it off by <u>heart</u>, because there's not so much to remember. Or forget...

A Summary **has all the** Main Points

You can use key words and phrases from any piece of writing to write a <u>summary</u>. A summary can be notes or proper sentences — it tells you the main points of the piece of writing as briefly as possible.

no, not summ<u>er</u>y...

Chubb — they know all about keys...

Nobody could expect you to remember something word for word. If you write the main points as <u>notes</u> it helps you to <u>understand</u> what it's all about — and it helps you to <u>remember</u> it, too.

Skim Reading and Scanning

This page will save you a lot of <u>time</u> and <u>effort</u>. You <u>don't</u> always have to read every little thing in <u>detail</u> — which is a good thing if you ask me.

Skimming is reading for a Rough Picture

Skim reading gives a <u>rough idea</u> of what a text is about. It's like looking at something quickly and having a <u>blurred</u> picture of it in your head. Look at it carefully, and you get more detail.

It's a bit like this.

You can see a rough picture of everything that's there.

Read the writing <u>quickly</u> and just <u>grab</u> the <u>key</u> points.

Scanning is reading for Key Words

When you want to <u>find</u> something in an index, it's much <u>quicker</u> to let your eyes wander over the page on the <u>lookout</u> for the word you want.

If you had to read <u>every single</u> word before you found the thing you wanted, it'd take <u>ages</u>.

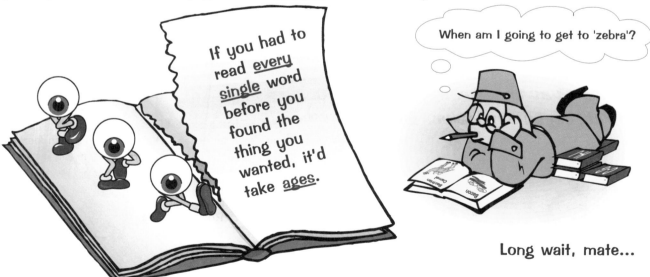

When am I going to get to 'zebra'?

Long wait, mate...

I scanned the barcode on the skimmed milk...

Finally, something you'll be <u>happy</u> to learn — you <u>don't</u> always have to read every little detail. Sometimes all you need to do is <u>skim read</u> to get the <u>important</u> bits. If you're looking for a particular subject just <u>scan</u> through until you find the <u>word</u> you are after. It all saves time.

Rhyming

Rhyming is pretty darn important in <u>poems</u>. The first rhymes you heard were probably in <u>nursery rhymes</u>, but loads of <u>pop songs</u> use them too. Time to see how it all works...

Words Rhyme if their Endings sound the Same

Words that have the <u>same ending</u> rhyme. Rhyme is used a lot in poems, but poems don't have to rhyme.

Little Bo Peep has lost her sheep.

These words rhyme. They have the same "-eep" ending.

frown, down, clown, town

These words rhyme. They have the same "-own" ending.

late, straight, mate, plate, eight

The endings don't have to be spelt the same way. They just have to <u>sound</u> the same.

A Rhyming Couplet is Two Lines that rhyme

If a line of poetry <u>rhymes</u> with the <u>next</u> one, you've got a <u>rhyming couplet</u>. Lots of poetry is made of rhyming couplets.

Gazing at the ocean
Putting on sun lotion.

Ocean rhymes with lotion.

Ring a ring of roses
A pocket full of posies.

Roses rhymes with posies.

It isn't such an exact rhyme, this time.

Learn to rhyme — you know you've got time...

You can't always tell which words rhyme just by <u>looking</u> at the <u>spellings</u>. You do actually have to say them out loud to yourself. <u>Couplet</u> means it's two lines — a <u>couple</u> of lines, if you like.

Verse, Chorus and Stanza

Many poems and songs are divided up into <u>verses</u> and <u>choruses</u>. You might have heard of them before, but now you've got a posh <u>new word</u> to learn — "stanza".

A _Verse_ is a _Section_ of a poem

A group of lines in a poem or a song is called a verse.
The verses in a poem have <u>different</u> words, but they follow the <u>same pattern</u>.

Verse 1) She'll be coming round the mountain when she comes,
   She'll be coming round the mountain when she comes.
   She'll be coming round the mountain,
   Coming round the mountain,
   Coming round the mountain when she comes.

chorus: Singing aye, aye, yippee, yippee aye, etc

Verse 2) She'll be wearing pink pyjamas when she comes,
   She'll be wearing pink pyjamas when she comes...

A _Chorus_ goes _Between_ the _Verses_ in a poem

The verses in a song or a poem are different.
The chorus is always the <u>same</u>, and it goes <u>between</u> all the verses.

This is the chorus. It goes between the verses in the song and it always stays the same.

Singing aye, aye, yippee, yippee aye.
Singing aye, aye, yippee, yippee aye.
Singing aye, aye, yippee,
aye, aye, yippee,
aye, aye, yippee, yippee aye.

You get the idea...

Stanza _is another word for Verse_

A stanza is a group of lines in a poem. The pattern of <u>syllables</u> and <u>rhyming</u> is the same for all the stanzas in the poem.

STANZA MEANS VERSE

Everyone join in with the chorus...

You'd think they'd be happy calling a verse a verse and a chorus a chorus, but no, they have to throw in this word "<u>stanza</u>". Don't worry about it, it's just another word for a verse in a poem.

Syllables

Short words are no problem to say, but long ones are more tricky — it's easier to think of the words split up into separate _beats_. Syllables are important in _poetry_, too.

Words _are_ Split _up into_ Syllables

Each bit of a word that's got a _separate sound_ is called a _syllable_.
A _syllable_ is like a beat in music. You could clap your hands once for each syllable.

You could put _trum-pet_ instead, it's just the same.

Trump-et

This word has _two_ beats — one for _trump_ and one for _et_. So it has _two syllables_. Easy.

The _only_ tricky thing about _syllables_ is the _name_.

Jester has _two_ syllables as well.

jest-er

Archery has _three_ syllables. You get the idea.

Arch-er-y

Syllable Patterns _are used in_ Poems

When _each line_ of a poem has a certain _number of syllables_, that's a _syllable pattern_.

The _syllable pattern_ of this poem is 7, 6, 8, 6.

1 2 3 4 5 6 7
Mary had a little lamb,   **7** syllables

1 2 3 4 5 6
It had a sooty foot;   **6** syllables

1 2 3 4 5 6 7 8
And into Mary's bread and jam   **8** syllables

1 2 3 4 5 6
Its sooty foot it put.   **6** syllables

Silly bulls — and silly cows...

This stuff is really important when you're _looking_ at poems or _writing_ your own. The _pattern_ of _syllables_ often repeats for each verse. When you're _reading_ long words, break them into syllables.

SECTION SEVEN — POETRY

Cinquains and Haiku

Don't worry, these funny looking words are just names for two more <u>types of poem</u>.
The big thing about both of them is the number of <u>syllables</u> that they've got to have.

Cinquains have a 22 Syllable Pattern

<u>Cinquains</u> are poems which always have the same <u>pattern</u> of syllables.
They have <u>five</u> lines which don't rhyme and have <u>22 syllables</u> altogether.
The syllables are in a 2,4,6,8,2, pattern.

Number of syllables

Summer: — 2

Sun shines so hot. — 4

Cat stretches in the heat, — 6

Dog lies down under cool tree shade, — 8

To sleep. — 2

five lines

The Haiku is a Japanese type of Poem

<u>Haiku</u> are short poems with seventeen syllables. They only have
<u>three lines</u> and their syllables always follow a 5,7,5 <u>pattern</u> like this:

Number of syllables

Small blushing flowers — 5

Float softly down from the trees; — 7

Cherry blossom time. — 5

three lines

Haiku are nice and <u>easy</u> to
write, because they're so <u>short</u>
and they <u>don't</u> have to rhyme.

Haiku — bless you! Have a tissue...

These poems don't have to rhyme. The number of <u>syllables</u> in each line is what's <u>important</u>.
Remember how many <u>lines</u> each kind of poem must have: cinquains have 5; haiku have 3.

Jingles and Nonsense Poems

These two really are fun. You probably know tons of jingles from <u>adverts</u> on the telly. <u>Nonsense</u> poetry makes you laugh — the sillier the better.

Jingles <u>get</u> <u>Stuck</u> <u>in your mind</u>

Jingles are short <u>catchy</u> poems used for advertising. You might not think of them as poems, but they use a lot of the same <u>word tricks</u> as poetry. They're written to stick in your head so you'll remember the product they are selling.

Mustard custard — it's a *specially spicy spoonful.*

This is <u>rhyme</u>, see P.36.

This is <u>alliteration</u>, see P.18.

Twice as nice and full of spice.

Here's another one that rhymes.

Nonsense <u>poems</u> <u>Play</u> <u>with</u> <u>Words</u>

You guessed it — <u>nonsense</u> poems are full of nonsense. They use <u>made-up</u> words that are fun to read. They talk about silly, loony stuff or impossible things happening.

Nonsense poems are written to make you giggle.

It makes no sense...

I am a silly fellow,
I'm Fred Ferknackerpan,
I wear one shoe that's yellow
and one that's toast and jam.
My wife just shakes her head
And says I am a loon.
I put hedgehogs in her bed
And flew it to the moon.

Nonsense? All a lot of rubbish if you ask me...

You don't need to know <u>why</u> a jingle's called a jingle. All you need to bother yourself with is what one is and what it's for. <u>Nonsense</u> poems are good clean fun, and well worth knowing about.

Calligrams and Shape Poems

Calligrams and shape poems aren't your run-of-the-mill everyday poems, that's for sure. They have added extras which make them eye-catching and fun.

Calligrams have Fancy Writing

Calligrams are poems that are written in fancy letters that have something to do with what the poem's about. You can really use your imagination here and come up with some hot letters, cold letters, fat letters, thin letters, scary letters...

On a cold, frosty morning,
My window is glazed with ice
In zigzag patterns like an Indian blanket.
Outside, leaves have thick white edges:
Spiders' webs are diamond jewelled.

This is written in frosty letters.

The pattern behind the words looks like ice.

Shape Poems are written in a Special Shape

The words in a shape poem are written into a shape that has something to do with what the poem's about.

It's about spiders, so it's written in a web — groovy.

Lucy spied a spider, lurking in her cider. With a frown, she drank it down, And now it lives inside her.

It's about pyramids, so it's written in the shape of one.

In
Egypt
Pharaohs
Built pyramids:
Palaces to be buried in.

Shape poems — Ode to a Triangle...

It's got to be said — good presentation really makes a huge difference. These two kinds of poetry really grab your eye — they're not just words thrown down on the page any old how.

Index

Index

Index